# Who Do You Say That I Am?

## A Man Called Jesus

Art and Text by
Robin Joyce Miller

# Who Do You Say That I Am? – A Man Called Jesus
## *Illustrations Inspired by Ethiopian Icons*
### Picture Book and Study Guide

*This book is dedicated to Pamela Chatterton-Purdy and the Rev. Dr. David A. Purdy.*
*Pamela suggested the title and inspired the poem.*
*David read the manuscript for accuracy.*

Published by Robin Joyce Miller

Copyright 2015 by Robin Joyce Miller
All rights reserved.
Published 2015.

ISBN 978-0-9828122-6-6

Robin Joyce Miller
email: rjmill1@aol.com

www.robinjoycemillerart.com

This book was designed and typeset by Nancy Viall Shoemaker of West Barnstable Press, West Barnstable, Massachusetts. The text font was set in Friz Quadrata. Initially designed by Swiss typographer Ernst Friz in 1965, the font was given its bold weight by Victor Caruso (1965) and its italic design by French designer Thierry Puyfoulhoux in 1992. *Who Do You Say That I Am* was printed on 100 lb. white matte coated.

# Who Do You Say That I Am?
## A Man Called Jesus

## TABLE OF CONTENTS

| | | |
|---|---|---|
| **I.** | **Poem: Who Do You Say That I Am?** Mark 8:29 | i |
| **II.** | **The Life of Jesus** | 1 |
| **III.** | **Seven Miracles of Jesus** | 11 |
| **IV.** | **The "I Am" Statements** | 18 |
| **V.** | **Study Guide and Meditation** | |
| | The Life of Jesus | 25 |
| | Seven Miracles of Jesus | 29 |
| | The "I Am" Statements | 31 |
| | Who Do You Say That I Am? | 34 |
| **VI.** | **About the Art** | |
| | Inspiration: Ethiopian Icons | |
| | Medium: Mixed Media Collage | 35 |
| **Notes** | | 36 |

# Who Do You Say that I Am?

Who do you say that I am?
Where am I in your life?
Do you feel my presence?
Do you see my light?

Are you always hungry?
Do you thirst for peace?
Do you need a shepherd?
Are you a long lost sheep?

Do you feel connected?
Does loneliness haunt your days?
Do you need to find a path
To guide you on your way?

Do you need to see my face?
Must you touch my hands?
Can you trust my promises?
Do you know my plans?

I have prepared a place for you
To sit right by my side.
A path to everlasting life
Where peace and love abide.

i

# The Magi, Mary and Baby Jesus

(Matthew 2: 1-12)

When Jesus was born, wise men, also called Magi, came to see him bringing special gifts.

The Life of Jesus

# The Baptism of Jesus

(Matthew 3:13-17)

Jesus was baptized by his cousin John.
He was declared God's son.

# Temptation of Jesus

(Matthew 4:1-11)

After fasting for 40 days and 40 nights in the wilderness, Jesus was tempted by the devil. He showed great faith and spiritual strength.

# The Beatitudes

(Matthew 5:1-12)

In the Sermon on the Mount, Jesus teaches his disciples and followers many important lessons about how God wants us all to live. He begins with the Beatitudes.

# The Lord's Prayer

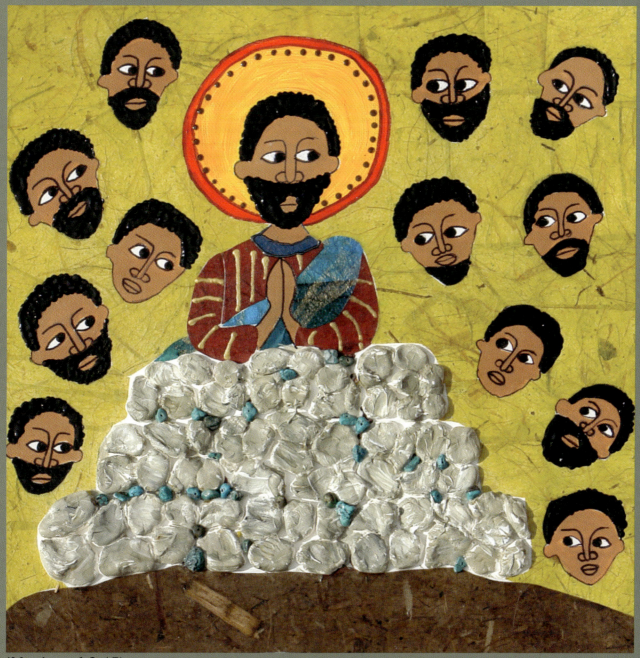

(Matthew 6:9-15)

Jesus taught us
how we should pray to God.

# Palm Sunday

(Matthew 21:1-11)

Jesus enters Jerusalem on a donkey. This day is referred to as Palm Sunday in many churches.

# The Last Supper

(Matthew 26:20-28)

Before Jesus' death, he has a Passover meal with his disciples. He explains the importance of this feast to them.
This gathering is commonly called The Last Supper, Holy Communion and the Eucharist.

# The Crucifixion

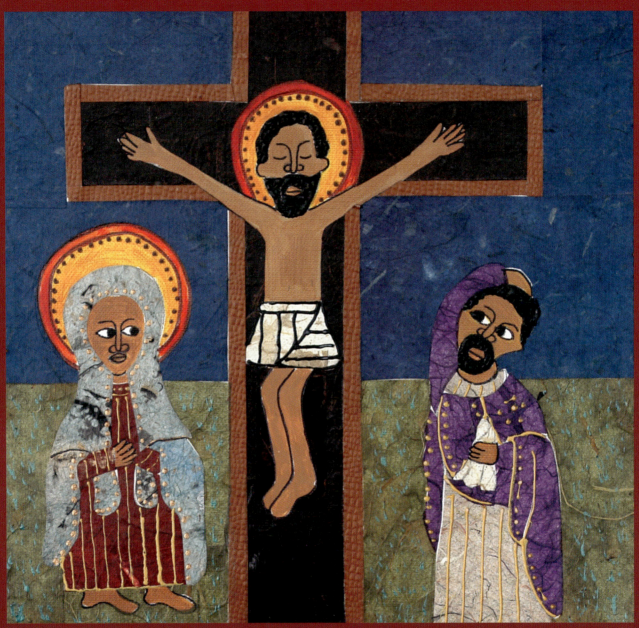

(John 19:26-27)

Jesus died a terrible death on the cross.
His mother, Mary, and the disciple he loved
are standing by him.

# The Resurrection

(Luke 24:1-6)

Jesus did not remain in the tomb.
When the women went to the tomb,
an angel told them that "He has risen".

# The Ascension

(Acts 1:1-11)

Jesus appeared to the disciples many times after his resurrection. After forty days, he ascended into heaven.

# Jesus turns water into wine

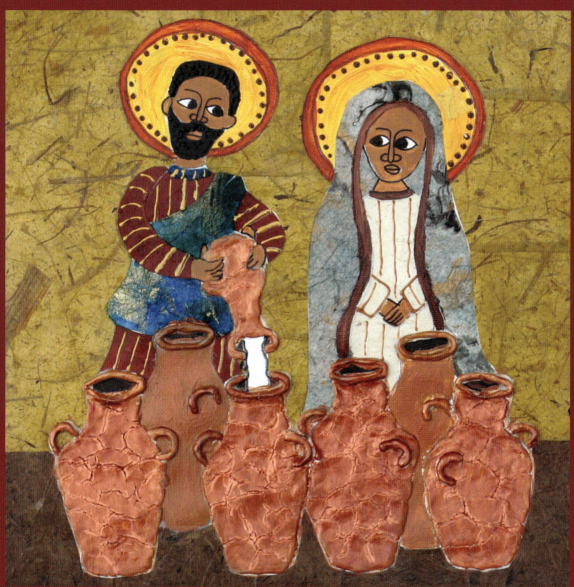

(John 2:5-11)

Jesus' mother, Mary, is with him when he performs his first of 37 miracles. There is a wedding taking place and they run out of wine. Jesus turns water into a superior quality wine.

Seven Miracles of Jesus

# Jesus heals the paralytic

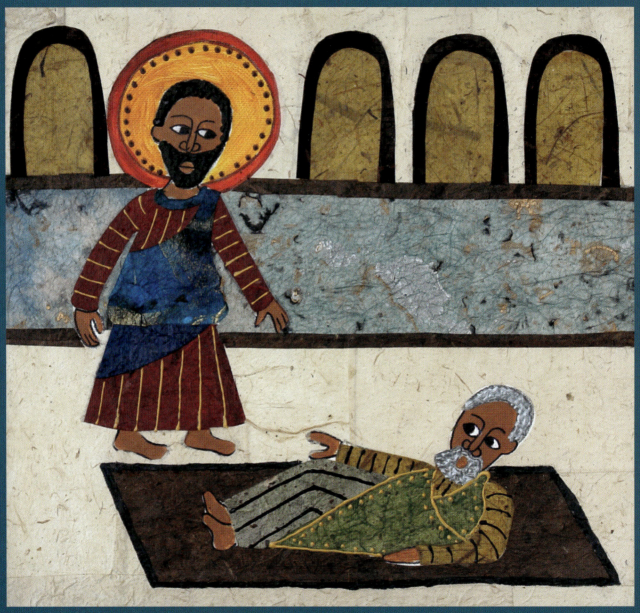

(John 5:2-9)

A man, lying by a healing pool, is unable to get in. Jesus speaks to him. Then restores his mobility. The man picks up his mat and walks away.

# Jesus heals the bleeding woman

(Luke 8: 43-48)

A woman, who has been suffering with a bleeding disease, touches the edge of Jesus' garment and is healed.

# Jesus feeds the multitude

(Matthew 14:13-21)

Jesus feeds 5,000 people with two fish
and five loaves of bread.

# Jesus walks on water

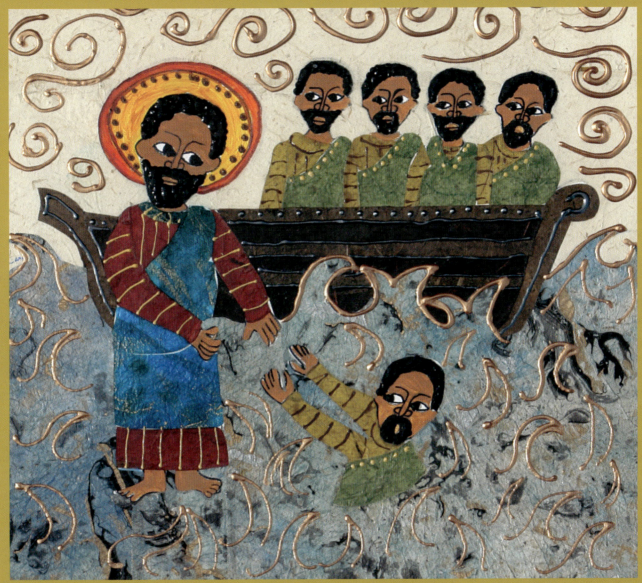

(Matthew 14:22-33)

Jesus gets Peter to walk on water. Peter focuses on the wind and rough water. Then he becomes afraid, loses faith and begins to sink. Jesus catches him and Peter gets back into the boat.

# Jesus heals the blind man

(John 9:1-12)

Jesus used his saliva to make mud to restore the sight of the blind man.

# Jesus brings Lazarus to life

(John 11:38-44)

A man named Lazarus has been dead for four days, when Jesus brings him back to life.

The "I Am" Statements

# I am the bread of life

(John 6:35)

If we come to Jesus, we will hunger for nothing. If we believe in him, we will never thirst.

# I am the light of the world

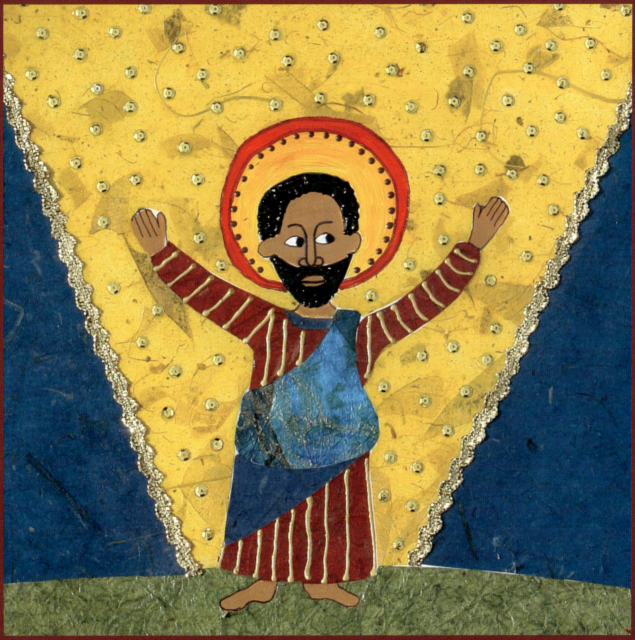

(John 8:12)

If we follow Jesus,
we will never walk in darkness.

# I am the gate

(John 10:9)

As those who enter a gate for protection,
Jesus will save those who enter through him.

# I am the good shepherd

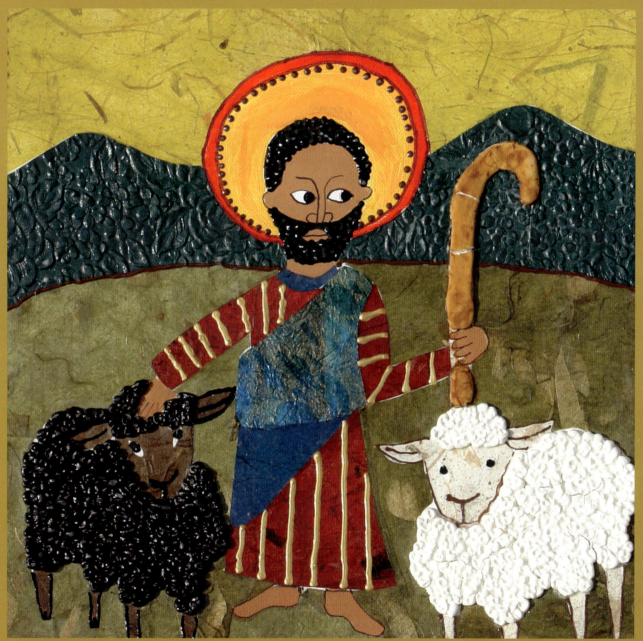

(John 10:11)

As a good shepherd would, Jesus will know and protect us. He will lay down his own life for us.

# I am the resurrection and the life

(John 11:25)

If we believe in Jesus,
we will have life even when we die.

# I am the way, the truth and the life

(John 14:6)

Jesus is the only path to God.

# I am the vine

(John 15:5-8)

We must stay connected to Jesus to be fruitful and have a good life. If we are not connected, we will not be able to function well in life.

# STUDY GUIDE
(Internet required to research some questions)

## - The Life of Jesus -

### The Magi, Mary and Baby Jesus
Bible Study: (Read Matthew 2:1-12)

1. Why did King Herod call the Magi secretly?
2. Did King Herod want to find Baby Jesus to worship him? What were the King's concerns?
3. Where else in the Bible was a great king concerned with the birth of a little baby?
4. What do we know about the background of the Magi?
5. How did the chief priests and teachers of the law know where the Messiah would be born? Read Matthew 2:4-6.
6. Did the Magi report back to King Herod? Explain.

*Meditation:*

1. Why do you think it is significant that Jesus was born to such humble beginnings? What is God telling us? What does this mean to you?
2. Have you ever been concerned that someone was going to take your position on a job, or outshine you in some way? How did you feel? How did this feeling affect your behavior?
3. What is it like to have a new baby in the family? Does everyone always celebrate?

### The Baptism of Jesus
Bible Study: (Read Matthew 3 and John 1:15-36)

1. Who was John the Baptist?
2. How did John identify himself when messengers from the Pharisees questioned him?
3. How does the bible describe him?
4. Though John the Baptist and Jesus were cousins, they didn't meet until the day that he baptized Jesus. How did John recognize Jesus when they first met? (Read John 1:29-34)
5. Why did people come to John to be baptized? Was Jesus the typical person that John baptized?

*Meditation:*

1. What does baptism mean to you?
2. What do you think about babies being baptized?
3. Were you baptized with water sprinkled on your head or submerged in water? Do you think the ceremony makes a difference?

## Temptation of Jesus
Bible Study: (Matthew 4:1-11)

During the temptation of Jesus, both Jesus and Satan quote scripture. Find the scriptures in the Old Testament for the following:
1. 'Man shall not live on bread alone, but on every word that comes from the mouth of God.'
2. 'He will command his angels concerning you.'
3. 'Do not put the Lord your God to the test.'
4. 'Worship the Lord your God, and serve him only.'

### *Meditation:*

1. Have you ever fasted? How did you feel?
2. Have you ever done anything for 40 days as a form of deprivation/sacrifice? Did it make you feel strong or weak?
3. Think of a time when you were tempted to do something you knew was wrong. Did you give in to temptation? If you remained steadfast, what gave you strength?
4. Jesus was well versed in scripture and was ready when Satan tempted him. Do you know enough about what is written to give you strength in difficult times?
5. Have you had a difficult experience that you could liken to being in the wilderness? Discuss it.

## Sermon on the Mount/Beatitudes
Bible Study: (Read Matthew 5:1-12)

1. Who was Jesus speaking to?
2. What does the word "Beatitude" mean?
3. What does blessed mean?
4. There are two parts to the Beatitudes, what are they?
5. Why are the Beatitudes important?
6. What does it mean to be poor of spirit?
7. Jesus often said things that were counter to society and the way people think. Would you think that you were blessed if: You are poor of spirit, mourn, are persecuted and insulted? What is Jesus telling us?
8. Name some characters in the Bible who hungered for righteousness. What was their reward?
9. Name some characters in the Bible who showed mercy.

### *Meditation:*

1. Do the Beatitudes bring you comfort? Explain.
2. Have you ever asked for mercy or been merciful to someone else?
3. Are the characteristics of the beatitudes easy to put into practice?
4. Why do we need to be peacemakers?

## Jesus Teaches Disciples to Pray (The Lord's Prayer)     Bible Study: (Matthew 6:5-15)

1. Jesus warns about not praying like the hypocrites. What does it mean to be a hypocrite?
2. Why should you pray in private?
3. Does Jesus mean that you should never pray in public?
4. Why is forgiveness so important?
5. Though many people end the Lord's Prayer with, "For thine is the kingdom and the power and glory forever", is it found in all bibles?

### *Meditation:*
1. Do you recite the Lord's Prayer as a rote memorized speech? Is that what Jesus wants us to do?
2. Do you need fancy words to pray to God?

## Jesus Enters Jerusalem     Bible Study: (Read Matthew 21:1-11)

1. What does "Hosanna" mean?
2. What is another name for Palm Sunday?
3. What words are used instead of "palms" in Matthew 21:1-11?
4. What did palms symbolize?
5. Where are the words "palm branches" mentioned in the Bible?
6. Matthew 21:4-5 speaks of the fulfillment of prophesy. Where is this prophesied in the Old Testament?
7. Why were the people cheering for Jesus? What did they want him to do?

### *Meditation:*
Jesus went from the highest praise to death within a week.
1. Have you had days when you were honored and celebrated?
2. Have you had days when you felt that friends or family turned against you?

## The Last Supper     Bible Study: (Read Matthew 26)

1. People have asked "What kind of bread did Jesus serve at The Last Supper – leavened or unleavened bread?" There are questions around this issue. Research it.
2. What is the relationship between Communion and Passover?
3. What is the significance of the body and the blood in Communion? Why do you think Jesus decided on those two things?
4. What did Jesus and the disciples sing at the end of The Last Supper?
5. What happened to Judas Iscariot? (Matt. 27:1-10)

### *Meditation:*
1. How would you feel knowing that you are at the last meal with your beloved mentor who is about to be killed?
2. Discuss the fact that Judas betrayed Jesus even after Jesus said, "But woe to that man who betrays the Son of Man! It would be better for him if he had not been born."
3. Have you ever done something that you knew would have severe consequences?

## The Crucifixion       Bible Study: (Read John 19)

1. Who was the disciple standing nearby?
2. What time was Jesus nailed to the cross?
3. What is the significance of the hours 12 – 3?
4. Jesus creates a new family at the cross. Explain.

*Meditation:*

1. Why do you think there was only one disciple at the cross?
2. Mary was a dutiful mother; she was with her son from the beginning to the end. Do you think Mary trusted that her son would be resurrected?
3. Do you trust God's word all the time? When do you have doubts?
4. Mary was given to the disciple that Jesus trusted and loved. How do you think Mary felt about this? How about the disciple?

## The Resurrection      Bible Study: (Read Mark 16:1-8)

1. Who were the first ones to arrive at the empty tomb?   Why were they there?
2. Who did the risen Christ appear to first?

*Meditation:*

1. When the eleven disciples heard that Jesus had risen, why do you think they didn't believe it? Hadn't Jesus told them that he would? Do you think you would have believed?

## The Ascension      Bible Study: (Read Mark 16:9-20)

1. What was Christ doing before he ascended into heaven?
2. What does it mean to sit at the right hand of God? Why is that important?
3. Pentecost is part of the Jewish and Christian faith. What does pentecost mean to Christians? (Research and read Acts 2)

*Meditation:*

1. What would you expect, if you sat at the right hand of God?
2. It says that Jesus was taken up into heaven. Who do you think took him?

# – Seven Miracles of Jesus –

### Jesus turns water into wine
Bible Study: (Read John 2:1-11)

1. This is the first of 37-recorded miracles performed by Jesus in the New Testament. What were some of the many other miracles?
2. How did Mary know that Jesus could perform this miracle?
3. Jesus reveals this miracle to only a few people, who are they?

*Meditation:*

1. Mary was acting like a typical mother here. Explain.
2. This was Jesus' first miracle. Do you think it was his most powerful and significant? Explain.
3. Why do you think Jesus performs his first miracle after he said, "My hour has not yet come"?

### Jesus heals the paralytic
Bible Study: (Read John 5:1-18)

1. How did Jesus disregard the law with this miracle?
2. What does Jesus think is more important than the law?
3. Is Jesus gentle with the paralytic?
4. The King James Version said that an angel came down at certain seasons and troubled the water. What does it mean to trouble the water?

*Meditation:*

1. What Negro Spiritual talks about troubling the water?
2. Would you go to a pool to be healed?

### Jesus heals the woman with internal bleeding
Bible Study: (Read Luke 8:43-48)

1. What was happening at the time of this healing?
2. Did Jesus approach the woman?
3. How do we know that Jesus is aware of this woman before he sees her?

*Meditation:*

1. Have you ever felt that Jesus was aware of you? How could you recognize this?
2. What can we learn from this woman's faith?
3. Do you need to actually touch Jesus to be changed, healed or faithful?

### Jesus feeds 5,000
Bible Study: (John 6:5-14)

1. Do the disciples think that feeding the crowd is possible?
2. Why does Jesus ask the question, "Where shall we buy the bread for these people to eat?"

*Meditation:*
1. The disciples seemed to have forgotten the powers that Jesus has already displayed. Why is it so difficult for them to believe that this can be resolved?
2. How often do you forget what God has done for you in the past, when a new problem comes along?

## Jesus walks on water                    Bible Study: (Matthew 14:22-33)

1. Before Jesus came to the boat to meet up with the disciples, what had he been doing?
2. Why didn't the disciples recognize Jesus when he walked on the water?
3. Why did Peter begin to sink?
4. What is the source of Jesus' strength? How can we attain that kind of strength?

*Meditation:*
1. When do you feel like you're sinking? What do you do?
2. How does this story give you hope?

## Jesus heals the blind man                    Bible Study: (John 9:1-12)

1. What do the disciples think is the cause of the blind man's condition?
2. What is Jesus' explanation for why the man is blind?
3. What did Jesus mean when he said, "As long as it is day, we must do the works of him who sent me. Night is coming, when no one can work?"

*Meditation:*
1. How should we feel and what should we do, when we see a person suffering?
2. How do you feel about people with sexually transmitted diseases?
3. When Jesus touched the man, he was not easily recognized by his neighbors. How can Jesus touch you in a way that people may not recognize you?

## Jesus brings Lazarus to life                    Bible Study: (John 11:1-44)

1. What does the name Lazarus mean?
2. When Jesus heard about Lazarus' illness, Jesus said, "This illness does not lead to death. It is for the glory of God, so that the Son of God may be glorified through it." What did he mean?
3. What did the resurrection of Lazarus represent for us all?
4. Why did Jesus cry, if he knew that he would raise Lazarus from the dead? What could he have been thinking about?

*Meditation:*
1. Jesus did not respond when Martha wanted him to, but how does this story end?
2. Does God respond when you want him to? How can this story gives you hope in your life and death?
3. There were many people in this story who did not believe this miracle was possible. How does this story affect your personal faith?

# - I Am Statements -

## I am the bread of life
Bible Study: (Read John 6: 25-59)

1. What interesting things happened in the beginning of this chapter? How do they relate to Jesus' "I am" statement?
2. Why does Jesus admonish the people who are following him?
3. What bread is Jesus talking about?
4. What is Jesus always trying to get people to think about?
5. Why did the Jews have difficulty believing that Jesus was sent from heaven by God?
6. What did Jesus say that was hard for even the disciples who knew and loved him to digest?
7. What ceremony honors this teaching that Jesus is the bread of life?

***Meditation:***
1. Why do we need bread? How is that like needing Jesus?
2. What do you hunger and thirst for?
3. Like the disciples, would it have been difficult for you to accept the words Jesus spoke about his body and blood?

## I am the light of the world
Bible Study: (Read John 8:12)

1. What kind of light and darkness was Jesus talking about?
2. What does it mean to walk in the light? Darkness?
3. What do you have to do to follow Jesus?
4. What promise does Jesus make?

*Meditation:*
1. When have you felt like you were walking in the light? The darkness?
2. What do you do to avoid taking a spiritually dark walk?
3. What do people see when you are walking in the light?

### I am the gate or the door         Bible Study: (Read John 10:1-10)
1. What does Jesus call those who he says will try to enter the kingdom by another way?
2. Who do the sheep listen to? Why?
3. Jesus was talking to the Pharisees, but they did not understand him. Who were the Pharisees?

*Meditation:*
1. What connections can you make between John 10 and Psalm 23?
2. What kind of relationship does Jesus want to have with us?

### I am the good shepherd         Bible Study: (Read John 10: 1-21)
1. Jesus makes many relationship comparisons. Explain.
2. Research the nature and ways of sheep.
2. Research the relationship between shepherds and their sheep.
3. Why should you put your trust in Jesus?
4. What makes Jesus credible?
5. Read John 10:22-40. Many people did not believe Jesus, why do you think this was so?

*Meditation:*
1. How can reading John 10 bring you comfort?
2. When have you felt like a sheep?
3. When have you shepherded someone?
4. What makes you feel safe?

### I am the resurrection and the life         Bible Study: (Read John 11:17-27)
1. What were the circumstances that prompted Jesus to make this statement?
2. What makes this "I am" statement so believable?
3. What statements do the disciples make that demonstrate that they still don't understand Jesus?

*Meditation:*
Many people fear death of self and loved ones.
1. How can this scripture be comforting?

## I am the way, the truth and the life     Bible Study: (Read John 13:31- John 14)

As Jesus discusses his departure, we can see that the disciples begin to get very anxious. Jesus tells them things to comfort them.

1. (John 13: 31-38) As usual, the disciples were a bit confused by Jesus' statements. What did Peter want to know?
2. What did Peter learn about himself?
3. What was the question that prompted this I am statement? Who asked it?
4. Jesus' statements and who he is could be very difficult for a person to comprehend. Did the disciples fully understand who Jesus was? Explain.
5. Why do Christians pray in the name of Jesus?
6. Did Jesus speak on his own behalf?

*Meditation:*

1. Jesus spoke a great deal about his relationship with God and man. What do you believe your relationship with Jesus is now? Has it changed over time?
2. Do you ever feel that the Holy Spirit is with you?
3. Do you feel a sense of comfort by the words Jesus spoke in John 14? Explain.
4. How does Jesus show you the way, the truth and the life?

## I am the vine     Bible Study: (Read John 15:1-17)

1. In this metaphor, who is God and what are we?
2. What is Jesus asking us to do in plain words?
3. What are the benefits for following his words?
4. If you choose not to follow Jesus' directive, "Remain in me", given in John 15, how could it be detrimental to you?
5. What does it mean to bear fruit?

*Meditation:*

1. If you are gardening and your job is to prune off dead branches, how do you know which branches to prune?
2. What did you do with the dead branches?
3. Have you ever felt disconnected from a friend or close relative? How did you function during those times?
4. What do you need to do to stay connected to Jesus, with so many worldly things happening all around you?

# - Who Do You Say That I Am? -

1. Why did Jesus ask the question, "Who do you say that I am?" What was happening at the time? Read Mark 8:27-29.
2. Who answered the question and what did that person say?

**Meditation:**

Read the poem. (page 1)

1. How might you respond to some of the questions posed in the poem?
2. The poet is not talking about food in the question - "Are you always hungry?" What else could someone hunger for?
3. Do you know the promises that Jesus has made in the Bible?
4. Part of the poem refers to the disciple, Thomas. He needed to see and touch Jesus in order to believe in his resurrection. Do you understand his doubt?
5. What questions or doubts might you have?
6. Who was Jesus . . . to the disciples? to the people he addressed? to those he helped and healed? Who is Jesus to you?
7. Now that you have completed the study and reviewed the significant events in Jesus' life, who do you say Jesus is?

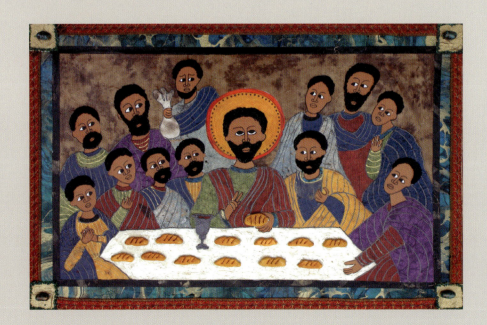

# About the Art

The illustrations are mixed media collages. Twenty-two of the illustrations are on canvasette. The Last Supper was rendered on canvas. Most of the work is done with decorative paper. Other materials used are acrylic, beads, gimp braid edging, Crayola® Model Magic®, fabric paint, thread, wheat and marker.

## Inspiration: Ethiopian Icons

The five authentic folk art icons below were used to inspire and capture the essence of the Ethiopian style that flows throughout the book's illustrations.

Ethiopian icons are brilliantly colored depictions of bible stories. They can be painted, carved, embroidered, cast in metal, or done as a wall mosaic. Icons can be made of wood, stone, paper, leather, etc.

# NOTES